Meet the Unicorns

Written by Alexandra Robinson

Illustrated by Shannon Hays

make
believe
ideas

Letter to Parents

Dear Parents,

This book is an engaging early reader for your child.
It combines simple words and sentences with delightful
illustrations of unicorns. Here are some of the many ways
you can help your child learn to read fluently.

Encourage your child to:
* Look at and explore the pictures.
* Sound out the letters in unknown words.
* Read and reread the text.

Look at the pictures
Make the most of each page by talking about the pictures
and identifying sight words. Here are some questions
you can use to discuss each page as you go along:
* Do you like this unicorn?
* What do you like about it?
* What is the unicorn doing here?
* Which unicorn would you like to meet? Why?

Look at rhymes
Many of the paragraphs in this book are simple rhymes.
Encourage your child to recognise rhyming words.
Try asking the following questions:
* What does this word say?
* Can you find a word that rhymes with it?
* Look at the endings of the rhyming words. Are they
  spelt the same? (Some are spelt the same, but not all.
  For example, "wood" and "good", and "you" and "true".)

Test understanding

It is one thing to understand the meaning of individual words, but you need to make sure that your child understands whole sentences and pages.

* Play "spot the mistake". Read the text as your child looks at the words with you, but make an obvious mistake to see if he or she has understood. Ask your child to correct you and provide the right word.
* After reading the facts, close the book and make up questions to ask your child.
* Ask your child whether a fact is true or false.
* Provide your child with two or three answers to a question and ask her or him to pick the correct one.

Sight words

This page provides practice with commonly used words that children need to learn to recognise on sight. Not all of them can be sounded out. Familiarity with these words will increase your child's reading fluency.

Picture dictionary

This activity focuses on learning vocabulary relating to unicorns. All the words can be found in the book.

Make-believe quiz

This simple quiz will help you ascertain how well your child has understood and remembered the text. If your child cannot remember an answer, encourage him or her to look back in the book to find out.

Meet the Unicorns

Come and meet the unicorns.
They're friendly, sweet and fun.
You'll find them splashing in a stream
or playing in the sun.

Did You Know?

The unicorns love playing hide-and-seek because they can make themselves invisible.

Wish Upon a Horn

The unicorns have spiral horns
that give them magic powers
to grant your wishes every day
and fill green fields with flowers.

Did You Know?

The unicorns can use their magic powers to make raindrops sparkle like glitter.

Magical Manes

They love to plait and decorate
their soft and glossy manes
with diamonds, gems and pretty bows
or strings of daisy chains.

Did You Know?

The unicorns sprinkle magic dust on their manes to make them change colour.

Little Unicorns

You might find little unicorns
all gathered in a wood.
It's where they meet for magic school
and learn how to be good.

Did You Know?

At magic school, little unicorns learn how to use their magic horns to paint the sky blue.

The Royal Unicorns

These unicorns live far away
in castles made of jewels.
They all have chocolate fountains
and big, sparkly swimming pools.

Did You Know?

The royal unicorns decorate their crowns with crystals that they find in glittery caves.

The Rainbow Unicorns

These unicorns have rainbow wings
and gallop through the sky.
They paint pink clouds and rainbows
as they swoop and soar and fly.

Did You Know?

Their wings show the seven colours of the rainbow: red, orange, yellow, green, blue, indigo and violet.

The Flower Unicorns

In spring, the flower unicorns
are found near cherry trees.
They race across pink meadows
with the butterflies and bees.

Did You Know?

The flower unicorns add
a different sweet scent
to each type of flower.

The Sunshine Unicorns

These unicorns have magic hooves
that sparkle, gleam and glow.
They make the golden sun appear
in every place they go.

Did You Know?

You can hear the jingle of the bells on their golden necklaces whenever they are nearby.

The Water Unicorns

The playful water unicorns
make homes in secret caves.
They love to splash in waterfalls
and jump through clear, blue waves.

Did You Know?
These unicorns are friends with horned sea creatures called narwhals.

The Snowflake Unicorns

These unicorns wear cosy coats
in cold and frosty weather.
They love to skate on frozen lakes
and glide around together.

Did You Know?
The snowflake unicorns live in icy palaces on snowy mountaintops.

The Midnight Unicorns

When midnight strikes, these unicorns
can brighten up the night.
They use their horns to make the stars
and fill the sky with light.

Did You Know?
When wolves howl at night,
the midnight unicorns know that
it's time to create the stars.

The Dream Unicorns

These very special unicorns
are always there for you.
They listen when you're fast asleep
and make your dreams come true.

Did You Know?
The dream unicorns fly above homes at night to protect people from bad dreams.

Sight Words

Here are some sight words used in context.
Use other sight words from the border in
simple sentences of your own.

The unicorns **like
to play in the** sun.

They have
magic horns.

I would love **to see a** unicorn.

Picture Dictionary

Write the correct word under each picture
to create your own picture dictionary.

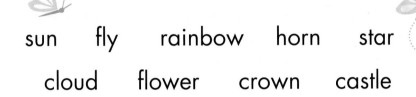

sun   fly   rainbow   horn   star

cloud   flower   crown   castle

Make-Believe Quiz

How much do you know about unicorns?
Circle the answers to find out. If you
can't remember an answer, look back
in the book.

1 What can the unicorns
do with their horns?

grant wishes   make cakes

2 What game do the
unicorns love to play?

I spy   hide-and-seek

3 Where do the royal unicorns live?

in castles   in caves

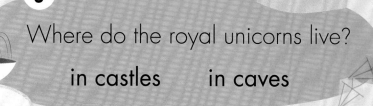

4 Who do the flower unicorns
like to race in pink meadows?
mice and squirrels
butterflies and bees

5 Where do little unicorns
meet for magic school?
in a wood   in a park

6 Who are the water
unicorns friends with?
rhinoceroses   narwhals

7 What do the midnight
unicorns do at midnight?
make stars   go to sleep

Find Your Unicorn Name

Find the first letter of your name. The word next to it is the first part of your unicorn name.

A: Sunshine	**J**: Silver	**S**: Magic
B: Cherry	**K**: Sunflower	**T**: Honey
C: Happy	**L**: Snowy	**U**: Bright
D: Midnight	**M**: Butterfly	**V**: Star
E: Glitter	**N**: Winter	**W**: Waterfall
F: Sweet	**O**: Pink	**X**: Twinkle
G: Daisy	**P**: Snowflake	**Y**: Bluebell
H: Crystal	**Q**: Blossom	**Z**: Cupcake
I: Meadow	**R**: Golden	

Find the month you were born. The word next to it is the last part of your unicorn name.

January: Dream	**July**: Berry
February: Rainbow	**August**: Dancer
March: Rose	**September**: Moon
April: Raindrop	**October**: Cloud
May: Flower	**November**: Sparkle
June: Summer	**December**: Jewel

Write your unicorn name here: